# GROWTH

........................................

KELSEY LONG

New Harbor Press
Rapid CIty, SD

Long/New Harbor Press
1601 Mt. Rushmore Rd, Ste 3288
Rapid City, SD 57701
www.NewHarborPress.com

Growth /Kelsey Long. -- 1st ed.
ISBN 978-1-63357-401-4

# INTRODUCTION

The Lord works in many ways, one of which being through nature. Whether taking notice of the entire galaxy or a faint blade of grass, it all reveals this delicate but powerful cycle that the world endures. Similarly, humans fall into this pattern too. We mourn, we rely, we persevere, we rejoice. Just like nature, I see in my own life that the Lord has paved out roads for me to travel and seasons for me to walk through. These seasons are not for me to approach on my own, but hand in hand with my Savior.

The seasons of my life that the Lord has guided me through are not always easy and are not always comfortable. Yet, they're also not always hard or complex either. There have been many sweet seasons of bliss, but also many tough seasons of discipline. So, although these are all different to some degree, there is always one truth about them collectively. They produce growth. Not perfection, as I so often try and appear to be in my own pride. Not shame, as I so often fall into without a full view of the gospel. Growth.

Like nature, the growth I have seen in myself does not occur in a day. It also does not occur in my own strength. Growth is a virtue that is a true and pure gift of grace from the Lord to give to me throughout every season. It leads to His glory and is not meant for me to collect my own false crowns. It results in my soul resting in fullness and security, knowing that my Father is in control and is ultimately good.

In order for growth to occur, there must be some kind of foundation that the plant will emerge from. Matthew 13 speaks to this too—this foundation of soil. The soil is the condition in which I am in when the Lord meets me and wants to grow me. Many times, I try to brush off my sin and act like I do not need to grow, but this is vanity. My soil is broken, my soil is in need, and the Lord does not see that and disregard me as unqualified for His love. He meets me in my mess, when I am feeling completely empty and without anything Godly or good in me, He does not leave me alone there.

Before a flower can be seen, a seed must be planted. Simple truth, really. Yet when the Lord grows a seed in my heart, it often falls on rocky soil because I disregard the truth that He is trying to kindly show me. From this blooms the lesson of seed. That, when I am without help and everything else has failed me, He is the one who faithfully rescues. That is where He sows the seed.

The planting is what comes after soil and seed. This is often the season I see His faithfulness and goodness, even though He has been growing me all along. This is where His grace is met with my hallelujah, and I can see that He has had a plan and it is better than mine. While He plants and continues to grow me, I rest fully and joyfully in dependence on Him because He is trustworthy and cares for me.

In this cycle of growth, there is the foundation of my soil, the lessons in the seeds He has sown, and the goodness of His planting. It does not end there though. These seasons He walks with me through and the ways in which He grows me are not just meant to grow me, but others. Nourish. Many of life's greatest lessons have come to me by someone else living them. The journey of life that I go through has unique lessons to be shared, and to nourish others. By sharing the Truth that the Lord has brought into our lives, we also share the growth He has brought as well.

All in all, growth is born from the different seasons that the Lord has walked with me throughout life. Soil, seed, plant, and nourish are seasons in this pattern that produce growth as He works through and in my soul. While each season has a different experience and lesson, none are without His grace or provision.

# REASONS FOR WRITING

There is nothing about me that is better than you. Let me make that clear. Without the Lord, I am broken. Through Jesus' life, death, and resurrection, I am redeemed. It is not from perfection that I am writing, or because I want to earn more love from the Lord. He loves all of His children with all that He has. His love is extravagant and not limited. It is unconditional, for you and for me.

On our best days and on our worst days, He is faithful in pursuit. I do not know where your soul is when you encounter this book. If you know and taste the goodness of the Lord, or if you just know Him by name. Still, I know and believe that He is chasing after you. Whether you feel emotionally like it or not, whether you feel like you deserve it or not, whether you care or not. He still cares for you. He always will, nothing you do can or will change this.

Many times, when I have been in the midst of writing, I approach it with my messy self. I have written when I felt far off or lost. If this is you, know that you are not alone in your mess. He often takes my mess and turns it into growth, and I have also written when I felt close to God and am learning much. This is the beauty in coming to Jesus, and in writing. I can bring my current state and remove the expectations that I easily pressure myself to live under. I can just be, and be with my Savior.

Writing has changed my life. I do not always love it, in fact sometimes I meet it with dislike. This is because writing forces me to process through things I would much rather skim over and move on from but need to process. When my head feels full of darkness, anxious thoughts, or intense emotions it allows me space to feel free and eventually come to see that all along I was never alone or without love.

I am told that I have a way with words
but it is much different than that
words have a way with me
running across my mind when i most need them
molding and shaping themselves into beauty
one sentence at a time
so call me an artist, call me a poet
but i only write them down
for it is them that works in me
   - poetry

That is the best way for me to describe the gift that writing is to me, through writing itself (ironic, right). If there is anything that I want you to hear through these words, it is that you are loved by the Lord, and He wants to grow you through His truth. I pray that this would be your takeaway above all else, and that this would ultimately be for His kingdom and His glory.

# CONTENTS

# ONE

......................................

# SOIL

Psalm 13:2
"How long will I store up anxious concerns within me,
agony in mind every day?
How long will my enemy dominate me?"

a heavy heart
(all I can give to You)
weighed down yet simultaneously drained.

*Growth*

your heart can't
heal,
mend,
learn,
grow,
if it's constantly being compared to those around you.

while on this Earth
(my temporary home)
there will be seasons, and there will be tides
magnetic magic that rushes me towards the shoreline
towards comfort,
and pulls me back out again, plunging into the deep
towards the unknown
this back and forth
is a consistent and persistent reminder
that growth isn't found in only one place
but rather the transition in between.

- tug of war

## Growth

I know not why
nor when or how
the trials come,

but as long as I remain here
on this planet as passing as the wind
they will come.

what Love is this
that even when I could give Him nothing good
nothing at all
that He still pursued me from mourning to dancing.

## Growth

I know -
that there is light at the end of this tunnel
that there is hope at the end of the journey
but what about right now?

do my present struggles go unseen?
how long will I fizzle and fade from the minds of all around
me?

yet He will hear me
in my aching
He will answer me
in my uncertainty

faithful He was, and faithful He is
whether in the midst of the deepest trial of the night
or the mercy flooding in throughout the morning
my redeemer will come to rescue me.

how long must I wait
in the in between of agony
how long must I wander
in the in between of realities
my soul stretches to heaven,
longing to be with You
but I am here.

You have me here.

and while I dwell here,
show me that I am not alone
show me that there is meaning here
for I only see seeds fallen on rocky roads
and hearts left in broken pieces
I desire to lift my eyes to You,
but lack the strength to do so.

   - be my strength + salvation

## Growth

God knows me fully
in all my joys
and in all my sorrows
yet He chooses to give me His victory.

- what I know and am still learning

(this is my broken hallelujah)
that He saw good in me when I was no good to Him.

# TWO

................................................

# SEED

Psalm 121:1-2
"I lift my eyes to the mountains. Where will
my help come from? My help comes from the
Lord, the Maker of heaven and Earth."

for the girl
falling asleep in her dorm room
(9 pm on a saturday)

you are still incredibly overwhelmingly enough
in a season where life demands adventure, freedom, and joy
in every moment
life is not made up of just the highs, nor is it just the lows
it is the seemingly mundane things that build discipline,
build character

so although this night may look different than social media
you are still where you are meant to be. where you need to
be.
and when that adventure, freedom, and joy is rooted in
knowing Jesus more deeply?
it will never run dry.

## Growth

you ask me to be the light,
but this sort of pressure can never be fulfilled

on my own, I cannot produce joy

but in Him, ships come home.

   - lighthouse

Jesus' love wasn't real to me,
until I was real with Him

when He removed my dirty cloths
and saw me in my sin and shame

He gazed upon me with intimate eyes
saying: *you are still worth going to the cross for*

it was then that I tasted the height and depth
of a grace that's wrapped in love

when He stayed, not only choosing the light in me
but the darkness

that is agape
and it is the faithful freedom I awake to.

   - in highest mountaintops and lowest valleys

## Growth

the looming tendency of abandonment reigns over my head
seasons shifting, people leaving, mysteries overwhelming,
with many drawn out goodbyes I gaze upon my past
eyes fixed on the consistent concept of change

the pressing anxiety of unknowns captivate my mind
growing older, stages transitioning, worry ensuing
with endless questions I wonder about the future
gaze set on the certain actuality of change

*look up, beloved*
the gentle and tender whisper puts an end to my spiral
it steadies and stills my soul,
what has happened is no longer of importance
what is to come holds diminished significance

for the One who has held every thought of mine
past and present and future
is here with me now,
and will be for all eternity

satisfaction, fulfillment, + meaning are found in the One
Who holds all things good and true
the reality is this: lifting my sight to the heavens
I see the one unchanging thing, God.

on my own, I am beyond weak
I fail to have even the slightest speck of love or wholeness
in my heart

this is why I must not start my days off with
checklists, post it notes, to-do lists, and reminders
but rather sit in simple silence
praying: *give me the desire to read more about You, Lord.*

## Growth

much like the seasons, we ebb and flow
drawn out and pulled back
restlessly wandering between war zones,
seeking and searching in the wrong settings and sites of the
world

this is not where we will be left though
for we will never truly be left,
as far as the east is from the west we are separated from our
iniquities
our cages, our shame, our captivity, our sins

for the Father's steadfastness is raw and real
each morning it is waiting for us
come back to this as your refuge,
come back to this as your home.

6:45 am wake ups call for
shuffling feet,
warm-to-your-core coffee,
rubbing eyes,
and a brilliantly vivid hello from the sun

but even when my eyes open, disoriented as to whether I
am in a dream or not
or my legs rise and bump due to the cold as I drag along to
class
I know that the joy given to me surpasses
any weariness from the day to day.

   - mercies new every morning

## Growth

You, my Savior, are not a stranger to loneliness
abandoned and denied
You have been rejected
so that I might be accepted
into an eternal bloodline thicker than anything I have known
with a love so redemptive it is sweeter than anything I have
ever tasted

Your lonely death, the finished work on the cross
is my only salvation
because You were raised to life
defeating death
defeating loneliness, defeating sin
You loved me enough to share this victory
(that I could never deserve and never earn)
with me.

Psalm 32:3

each day, awakening to various noises that filled an empty
void
shoveling bits and pieces of my soul until my cup ran dry,
I had poured and poured
but could give no longer.

Psalm 32:7

no, not by my own will
nor by my own way
nor with my own words
will I ever find freedom from what holds me so captive

my hiding place, my dependence
in You alone, I find such satisfaction
the One who took my pain and carried my burdens
trading it for His gifts, for Himself

every day coming across another struggle, temptation, ache
but ultimately knowing
not by me, but by Him
I am fulfilled.

*Growth*

some times,
some days,
are just like that
you can't please everyone:
you can't be everything to everybody
you can't say yes to every plan
your life wasn't made just for you to slave away for perfection

24 hours,
that's all you've got from morning to morning
so take a deep breath in,
and release it slowly
inhaling love
exhaling anxiety

there is provision here
even when you can't see it,
but more than what the past has held or the future will hold
there is grace here
in this very moment.

in the moments
when I can no longer keep my body above my feet
I lay myself to rest in the arms of my Father

my constant One
in whom I surrender and trust despite the shifting seasons
you carry me when I can't move any further

it is not me running back to Abba
but looking up and seeing Him running to me
tenderness within His eyes urging me to trust that *He is good*

God is no stranger to me
for His hands have holes from the very things
I try to mend the holes in my heart with

I count them all a loss in light of knowing Jesus Christ
(all the remedies i made for myself from pride)
nothing fulfills me like resting my spirit in His.

   - surrender

before You, I was seeking life from nothing more than
emptiness
licking a twisted version of love off knives
always left with the unsatisfying aftertaste of discontent-
ment in my mouth.

before You, I was wandering aimlessly, coming up hollow
time and time again
picked up and carried like the wind
never deeply rooted enough for life to grow inside of my
stone heart.

it is for this reason I am delighted when people tell me I
embody joy
reminding me, on my own I could never fake enough
"happiness"
but after You, I dance in the freedom of eternal bliss.

   *- coming to Jesus*

if they did not create you
they do not have the authority to define you.

- *imago dei*

## Growth

growth isn't a one-day process:
there are many things I wish I knew more of
and many I wish I knew less,
there is time spent creating community
and time spent in solitude,
there is time spent stumbling over the hassle of the
day-to-day
and time spent breathing in quiet stillness

whatever I do, there is still more to be done
but I know now that it is okay to not have everything fig-
ured out
I know now the value in saying "no"
I know now this thing, life, can't be rushed
can't be learned
in one day.

   *- for the eighteen year old girl*

alone,
doesn't feel lonely
when spent with the Maker of the heavens and Earth
doesn't feel isolated
when spent with the Maker of each intricate being
and doesn't feel empty
when spent with the Maker of my soul.

*Growth*

it may feel like you're being buried by your shame
but remember
when Jesus redeemed the world the picture of you in His
mind wasn't you smoothing out your sin by yourself
it wasn't you dusting off the dirty parts and putting on a
smile

it was you
so hopelessly broken, so desperately in need
it was you and every bad thing that comes with that
He came to redeem the world
He came to take you by the hand and show you a way
through
show you His light and love
show you to throw off your shame burying you and,
taking His hand,
come up from the grave.

there are journeys in this season
not meant to be trekked alone
but endured alongside those
who inspire you to live closer to Him

and when the road is narrow enough for only one?
let Him carry you.

## Growth

I chose to see victory
in the doubt, pain, uncertainty
I chose to see victory
in the frustration, hurt, bewilderment
I chose to see victory
not because of my present circumstances,
or mere optimism
I chose to see victory
because I know Who held yesterday
has today
and holds tomorrow
I chose to see victory
because the Way Maker knows what is to come
even when I do not
I chose to see victory
and I know I will see victory
because I chose to see God
and I know I will see God.

 - 2020

# THREE

...........................................

# PLANT

Psalm 84:10-11
"Better a day in Your courts than a thousand anywhere else. I would rather stand at the threshold of the house of my God than live in the tents of wicked people. For the Lord God is a sun and shield. The Lord grants favor and honor; He does not withhold the good from those who live with integrity."

let faith arise
for this is my prayer

conflicted and convicted I am found bound by chains
shackled by insecurity
caged by sin

yet because of the Lord's great love for me
that endures from this life onto the next
I will sing of Your faithfulness, even when I cannot feel its
nearness

freed by grace
released by mercy
salvation through the old rugged cross
victory from the empty tomb

let faith arise
for this is my prayer
that I may know Him more vastly, love Him more deeply
and dwell in His courts
for all my days.

*Growth*

body + soul
although my eyes cannot see, there is far more to me than
the skeleton and skin
at the intersection of two realities
eternity finding its home within my temporary bones

flesh + spirit
torn between distinct desires, the thorn in my side holding
me in bondage
tasting freedom yet knowing captivity
tug of war waging a battle, but the victory is already finished

earth + heaven
living amongst disease and death
yet knowing there is more beyond the horizon of this mi-
croscopic view of life.

- homesick for heaven

I prayed: *show me that You are faithful*
and He sent hardships to endure,
so I could see that He stood and strengthened me

I prayed: *teach me how to dance*
and He placed me in the fire
so I could see the joy and freedom in refinement

I prayed: *make me more like You*
and He took away my comfortability
so I could see His character behind my fear

all along, on this journey I have trekked
stumbling as I go
He has been patient to grow me

revealing that,
His greatest gifts are not packaged in pretty and pleasant things
but in the raw and chaotic seasons of life

as I walk through these times, I look beyond my present reality
to the future hope that one day
I will walk in the cool of the day with my Savior.

- answered prayers

## Growth

four seasons,
loyal and steady from one to another
breathe in each one,
slowly
sweetly

this change is inevitable
ebbing and flowing
planting and growing

so do not wish this away
you are where you are
(where you need to be)
there is meaning here

there will come a time
to cultivate
but before that season,
there is a time
to dig, to plant, to wait.

   - four seasons,
   one God.

this isn't a linear process
set all of the goals you want, but do so with grace
track your completion of them, but do so with compassion

knowing that,
there will be mountains, and there will be valleys
some days you will trek a mile forward
others you will only be able to stagnantly sit

and that's okay.

   - healing

a breath in
a breath out
to follow the world's pattern
of holding and releasing
as if somehow, someway
we might just make it
however confined we may be
breath is the one thing we are in control of.
I don't remember my first
and I may not know when it's my last
but for all the breaths in between
the ones on a simple winter night that stores wisdom
or within the soft hum of a summer night
whether I'm surrounded by loved ones
or basking in solitude
and for all the breaths taken away
by moments, people, places
of sadness or of joy, as I take part in the human condition
I know that Your breath has always,
and will always,
sustain me.

   - breath

we are His
and where we see pieces of broken clay
He sees redemption.

- potter + clay

# Growth

when I open my eyes, I wake up in grace
this is not a grace that is pretty and polished
no, it is not meant for my image to be elevated

this grace is deep-rooted
messy
tangled
steadfast

this is hard work
as well as *heart* work
trusting in the One who is my definer and refiner
abiding in His grace
His personal grace
that carries me through each intricate trial
(no matter how trivial)
of this day

and knowing that,
like manna,
it will be renewed and lavished on me
tomorrow
and for eternity.

a message I need to be reminded of every morning:
*you do not need to earn your Father's love.*

- who God is

*Growth*

in my years of study I fear to have lost the core of my Creator,
for what do I gain if I know more about theology than
character?
God wants me to sit with Him,
not merely slave away for Him
His central desire is not for my sacrifices and is not for my
good works,
but for my heart

and so I return, I come, I sit
with only my open hands and fragmented heart to give,
I raise my eyes in adoration to the Savior
and find that His delight has matched my gaze
saying: My attention has never departed from you,
neither has My love.

   - at the feet of Jesus

be patient with yourself,
knowing there is personal grace, truth, and mercy desig-
nated for you
to clothe yourself in every morning.

## Growth

a year ago, she did not know the trials to come
yet now a year later she has been refined and redefined
not by her own will
nor by her own way
but through The Way
Who holds a sacred will
she found growth

and so as she looks upon another year,
uncertainty overflowing and chaos ensuing
she trusts the faithful Author of life
Who has proven to be her peace time and time again.

a restless heart found it's dwelling in my own
spirals of comparison and bitterness encompassed my head
+ my hands attempted to do kingdom work from this
perspective,
from my own willpower

all the while, my sweet Savior set his gaze upon me
whispering: *you aren't made to do this life alone,*
*to carry these things alone*
*whispering: return to Me, beloved*

what a paradox this is
to live is for Christ, to die is gain
to be humble is to be exalted
and to die to self is to live

when my own willpower
my own hands, head, and heart failed
it was there that I found life
there that I found Jesus

so, in all my wandering
I have seen that there is nothing better than to return to
God
to lay down my life
and find freedom.

*Growth*

don't shy away from them
these hardships,
embrace them
and feel your way through them.
knowing that
(at the end of this journey)
you will see all along
that the One who created you
is the same One who sustained you.

- in the valley's + victories

Psalm 132:7

it is my joy
in the purest and most complete form
to sit at Your feet, crying *Abba*

there is beauty in surrender
not tangible or physical
but abounding in redemptive grace

it drips like honey
from the heavens
and even the nights I cannot taste its goodness
(especially the nights I cannot)
it is evermore lavished on me.

trapped in my fear
suffocated by my inadequacy
You met me there
when my praise was empty
and my own strength failed me
You met me there
the beautiful Savior and a restless wanderer met face to face
— The Father's pursuit unmatched as the mask melted away
my authentic and broken hallelujah I raised to You
to the One who met me with healing
this is the hallelujah that is more than good deeds and a checklist,
this is the hallelujah that is more than my worst hours and darkest moments,
this is the hallelujah inspired by The intimate God of creation
Who met me
Who continues to love me, however messy
+ Who desires to meet and love you.

though I do not know
what each season holds for me
how blissful the summer, how desolate the winter
I do know my God
and my God knows me

like a branch swaying in the restless wind
I toss and turn in all directions
yet can draw back to Him for security.

  - planted roots

# FOUR

........................................

# NOURISH

Psalm 63:3
"My lips will glorify You, because Your faithful love is better than life."

this gospel,
it was not set aflame just to sit idly in solitude
it's warmth was created to spread
like wildfire
overcoming and overwhelming
sparking other lights
to do the same.

   - the great commission

self-obsessed &
self-depressed.
I think it's time we all try selflessness
to rid of our own ways,
being buried in our own shame
and instead, be redefined by the trying of the times
when we think we've had enough
or we just don't measure up,
remembering how to love others
as if it were not our own life but our sisters and brothers,
a life to be lived in love for one another.

  - the selfless transformation

because when you meet Jesus—
you meet Love.
not the kind in the movies or the gaze from a mother to her
infant, those are mere glimpses
you meet the purest and truest Love in all existence and
eternity
the kind that is so infinite and unconditional that you want
to scream it from the mountains.

because when you meet Jesus—
you meet Life.
not the kind of short-lived laughter or genuine conversa-
tions that happen every once and awhile, those too are mere
glimpses
you meet the abundance and joy that lies within the mun-
dane and within the pain
the kind that is so everlasting and soul satisfying you want
to dance in the middle of a crowded room.

the kind of Love and Life that inspires coming to the feet of
Jesus and discovering what it means to be complete.

*Growth*

set your feet upon the foundation of unending love
grounded in unceasing redemption,
build your life around this identity
and when the enemy comes to wring out the good out of
the good news,
may you be found in Him again and again.

I wish for my life to be a mirror-reflection
not of my own heart
and not my own speech and conduct
but of that of the gospel

who am I to bring salvation to anyone?
it is not my power,
but rather my mission
to share with you the life that I have found,
the only life,
in Him alone.

*Growth*

how beautiful is it
that the Lord despises sin
but not me,
even when I choose the very thing that sent Him to the
cross

this is why I desire to die to my flesh
and no longer walk in those past ways of sin,
because God's abounding love places me
above His convenience and comfort.

from dust, from breath, from ribs
carefully and cautiously,
but with complete confidence
you came into existence

each intricate mark on your skin
is accounted for like the stars,
and out of all the beauty in this world
He chose you as precious in His sight.

  - Psalm 139

Light of the world
hope in the flesh
He came.
man from Heaven
obeying His loving Father's will
He came.
as vulnerable as a baby
born to die for us
He came.
rejected by innkeepers that night
rejected by us on the cross
He came.
and while the greatest human was being born
where were we?
He came.
in a manger
yet we were asleep
He came.
how often do we remain stuck in a coma
oblivious to Him, to GOD
He came.
so that we could wake up
and live in freedom
He came.
He lived. He died. He rose. He loves.

defined by and refined by the Creator:
where the world tells me I am merely flesh on bones
You tell me I am soul in body
not just a holding space for cells and genes
but a dwelling place for the Spirit of the Lord

where the world tells me I am insignificant and nameless
You tell me I was chosen from my mother's womb
not made just to measure up each day
but take refuge and rest in that Jesus already has on my
behalf.

## Growth

you are here
now
in this moment
for a reason, and for a purpose

it is not a mistake that you woke up today
it is not by accident that you are in the exact space you are
at the exact time you are

no one has the history you do,
and no one can tell your story like you
you can (and do) inspire and influence the world.

   - I'm sorry if no one has told you this before (that doesn't
mean it's not true)

like light
we can walk throughout this day
knowing the Father's face is never far from us

sun-streaked rays across the roads we will travel
are a reminder
*you are loved beyond all measure.*

## Growth

for God to be intentional
He must also be intimate,

He is not a mere observer, sitting above this minuscule
world
but rather a potter
choosing to stay in our lives, no matter the difficulty

it is not convenient for Him to love us
and yet He sacrificed everything
shaping and molding us along the journey to eternity.

in the steady beat of the tumbling snow
exquisite flakes of flurries fall
I think about them.
at first glance they seem so simple, so plain
but catching even just one, a wonderful surprise is revealed
I think about them.
there is so much more here than what meets the eye
hydrogen bonding takes place as they drift from the
stratosphere
I think about them.
each one, specific and unique
parallel to the 8 billion people dwelling on this planet
I think about them.
the distance some had to travel,
the ones who never do reach their place
I think about them.
the trillions of atoms that work in unison
just to keep one moving
I think about them.
what they are all doing right now
falling in love or falling asleep
I think about them.
maybe there is a greater connection between every human
than I have acknowledged until now
or maybe I'm just admiring hydrogen bonding on a
December night
I think about them.

- where my thoughts take me

# Growth

through the years God is still for me
He is the tender gaze in a new mother's eyes, He is the
steady ship in my crashing waves
to know Him is to love Him and to love Him is to live
what is my purpose aside from Him?
I am a mere vine, clinging onto the Branch + pressing into
the arms of her Father.

- faithful

there is no prototype for beauty
+ if there is: you are in it
how silly is it of us to think that we should should strive
only to be beautiful
to starve
to compare
to work to death
to tear down
you are a part of beauty, but you are much more
you are hurricanes and tornadoes colliding
you are earthquakes and tsunamis combusting
your mind is a galaxy
your body is a sanctuary
+ your soul is held sacredly within and for eternity.

when you realize that finding yourself, truly means
finding Jesus
then you learn what is means to
*come home.*

CPSIA information can be obtained
at www.ICGtesting.com
Printed in the USA
LVHW081633170921
698101LV00015B/1004

9 781633 574014